MAGIC CAT PUBLISHING

The illustrations were created digitally
Set in Abhaya Libre and Calder
Library of Congress Control Number 2024932981
ISBN 978-1-9155-6992-9

Book design by Stephanie Jones
Edited by Jenny Broom

First published in North America in 2024 by Magic Cat Publishing,
an imprint of Lucky Cat Publishing Ltd,
Unit 2, Empress Works, 24 Grove Passage, London E2 9FQ, UK

Printed and bound in Guangdong, China
1 3 5 7 9 8 6 4 2
Distributed by ABRAMS
195 Broadway, New York, NY 10007, USA

FSC www.fsc.org
MIX
Paper | Supporting responsible forestry
FSC® C122384

ABRAMS The Art of Books
195 Broadway, New York, NY 10007
abramsbooks.com

THE Birthday Music Book

Illustrated by

Amy Adele

MAGIC CAT PUBLISHING
NEW YORK

THE BLUE DANUBE

Composed by Johann Strauss II

Slowly, night gives way to dawn.
A little mouse wakes up and yawns.

Her whiskers twitch. She turns and blinks . . .
My birthday! Little Mousey thinks.

IN THE HALL OF THE MOUNTAIN KING

Composed by Edvard Grieg

Through her door come muffled sounds
As **furniture** is shuffled around . . .

Whispers . . . Footsteps cross the floor . . .
She slowly **peeks** outside her door.

PRELUDE

From Cello Suite No. 1 in G Major, composed by Johann Sebastian Bach

Her mother calls, "Good morning, dear!
But—stop! You mustn't come in here!

"Go outside and pick some flowers.
Come back home in half an hour."

Mousey wanders
through the woods.
The forest floor smells sweet
and good.

ODE TO JOY

From Symphony No. 9, composed by Ludwig van Beethoven

The flowers **flourish** in the sun.
She stops and stoops to sniff each one.

Through the air, the church bells chime.
She quickly **stops** to check the time.

Mousey, there's no time to wait:
Run back home—you can't be late!

Hop, skip, jump goes Little Mouse,

But as she steps inside the house . . .

OVERTURE FROM
THE MARRIAGE OF FIGARO

Composed by Wolfgang Amadeus Mozart

Mousey can't believe her eyes!
All her friends call out,
"Surprise!"

"THE CAN-CAN"

"Infernal Galop," from *Orpheus in the Underworld*, composed by Jacques Offenbach

She **blushes**
through her mousey fur,
For **everyone** is here . . . for *her*!

The **music** starts, excitement grows.
They **clap** their hands
and tap their toes.

HAPPY BIRTHDAY

Composed by Patty and Mildred J. Hill

A hush descends upon the room . . .
A cake with candles lights the gloom,

Then cheerful singing fills the house:
Happy birthday, Little Mouse!

ABOUT THE PIECES

1. The Blue Danube

"The Blue Danube," composed by Austrian Johann Strauss II in 1866, is a famous piece of music inspired by the Danube River. The music is a waltz: a dance where you sway side to side in triple time, counting 1-2-3. At first, the piece wasn't popular, but over the years it has become one of the best-known pieces of classical music ever written.

2. In the Hall of the Mountain King

"In the Hall of the Mountain King" is a piece of music by Edvard Grieg, a Norwegian composer and pianist. The music was inspired by another Norwegian, Henrik Ibsen, whose play *Peer Gynt* tells the story of a boy who sneaks into a mysterious king's realm. The music starts quietly and gets faster, making you feel like you're about to experience something exciting!

3. Prelude

Johann Sebastian Bach, a famous composer from Germany in the 18th century, wrote six Cello Suites between 1717-1723. This prelude opens Cello Suite No. 1 in G Major. It was rarely performed for more than two hundred years, but is now considered one of Bach's most important pieces of music.

4. Ode to Joy

"Ode to Joy" was composed by Ludwig van Beethoven in the early 19th century. It's part of his Symphony No. 9 in D minor. Beethoven was a brilliant composer from Germany who wrote this piece even when he was losing his hearing.

5. William Tell Overture

An overture is a musical introduction to an opera or ballet. The "William Tell Overture" was composed by Gioachino Rossini in the early 19th century. Rossini, an Italian composer, created 39 operas in his lifetime. This iconic piece came from his last one, which tells the story of a Swiss folk hero, William Tell.

6. Overture from The Marriage of Figaro

This piece of music opens *The Marriage of Figaro*, an opera composed by the famous Austrian composer Wolfgang Amadeus Mozart in the late 18th century. The opera is based on a comedic play and follows the escapades and intrigues of Figaro, a clever servant. It is thought of as one of the best operas ever written, full of lively comedy and memorable melodies.

7. "The Can-Can"

The real name of "The Can-Can" is "Infernal Galop," from Jacques Offenbach's operetta *Orpheus in the Underworld*. Around fifteen years after Offenbach died, this lively piece was played at Parisian cabarets the *Moulin Rouge* and the *Folies Bergère*, where dancers performed a high-kicking dance called the Can-Can to it. It has been informally known by this name ever since.

8. Happy Birthday

"Happy Birthday to You" is the most famous English song in the world. It was composed by Patty Hill and her sister Mildred J. Hill, two American schoolteachers, in the late 19th century. Originally, the song was titled "Good Morning to All" and was used to greet students into the classroom.